75
MESSAGES
DAILY THOUGHTS OF LIFE

BY REVEREND DOCTOR OGDEN L. KING II
WITH *SPIRITUAL GUIDANCE BY*
APOSTLE DR. ELBERT COLDEN INTRODUCT

This Book Is Dedication To:

My late parents Wilton & Lucille King Sr. for bringing me up in the Church. My late sisters Mildred Castille and Mary Ethel Charles, late Brothers Leroy Charles and Phillip L. Charles, oldest Nephew Merlin Guilbeau, my late Niece Susan Smith and my late host of Uncles and Aunties who watch over me while I was young and all of my friends who have pass this way and gone home.

I am the youngest of twelve brothers and sisters so I also would like to dedicate this to all my living Brothers and Sisters. For they have always watched over and protected me. I do not want to forget my wonderful Children, Nieces, Nephews, other Family members and Friends who have come to understand and respect the calling in my life. What a really big
family I have, I do know and I thank God for each and everyone of them.

Also, I would like to personally thank Mr & Mrs Charles and Jacqueline Long Manns for all the effort and time they put in this book.

REVEREND DOCTOR OGDEN L. KING II

ISBN: 978-1-961677-82-1 (Paperback)

Library of Congress Control Number:
2023919061

Printed in the United States of America

Published by:

info@thequippyquill.com
(302) 295-2278

About The Author

REVEREND DOCTOR OGDEN L. KING II

Was ordain and started preaching the gospel in 1999 at Believers For Christ Ministry; Walter Davis Sr., Pastor. He started evangelizing at various churches including New Life Church of GOD in Christ; the late Nathaniel D. Carter, Pastor. He also had the privilege to work under the late, Honorable Chief Apostle Fred Jacob out of Alexandria, Louisiana. Later, he became Assistant Pastor at Mt. Pleasant Baptist Church in Melville, Louisiana: Johnny Offord, Pastor.

The path to ministry for Rev. King was blessed with ups and downs, hardships, triumphs, illnesses, and Music. Music was always a dream of his. He is the youngest from a family of 12, where his parents raised them up going to Church every Sunday. At the age of 13, he began singing with a rhythm & blues (R&B) band called Merlin & The Superflies. At Opelousas Senior High School, Ogden played football, ran track and sang in the school choir. He graduated from high school and attended Delta Business College and Louisiana State University – Eunice. At LSU-E, he joined the SYNBADD BAND and started learning to play the bass guitar. Finally, he got the chance to play semi-pro football with the Lafayette Angels and later a failed attempt at NFL professional football.

However, after receiving a back and knee injury the football career idea was over. Ogden then returned to his first love, Music. With relatives and close friends, GRATITUDE BAND was formed. The band performed locally for a while then that led to the forming of G.K.G.L SPIRIT Gospel Group. He really enjoyed serving the Lord in song. For 18 years the group traveled, performed and recorded Gospel Music.

It was doing this time period that he decided to become a Minister. Rev. King recalls, "After we came home off tour one day, Elbert Bolden (a Minister at that time) came and prophesied to me and band member Kip Guilbeau. Pastor Bolden said that we're going to be working for the Lord someday. At that time, we didn't take it to heart. Now, just a few years later here we are both working for the Lord.

In 2006 Liberty Christian Center was born. Pastor Elbert Bolden asked Rev. King to come on board as his Assistant Pastor. In 2012, Rev. King became Pastor of the Center, under the Leadership of Apostle Dr. Elbert Bolden. In addition, in 2012, Rev. King studied at Andersonville Theological Seminary College and earned his Doctors Degree in Biblical Studies and Theology from Sacramento Theological Seminary College. He had already received his Masters in Biblical Studies (2004), Bachelor (2002) and Associate of Church Ministry Degree (2000) from The Sure Foundation Theological Institute College.

Today, the Reverend Doctor Ogden L. King II preaches the gospel of Faith and Prayer. He states, "GOD change me by Faith. He can change anybody if they are willing to be change by Faith." Rev. King wants all to know that, "There is power in prayer. Much prayers – much power. Little prayer – little power. No prayer – No Power!" (Amen.)

My Mentor
APOSTLE DOCTOR ELBERT BOLDEN

Apostle Dr. Elbert Bolden founded the Liberty Christian Center in June of 2006. Apostle Dr. Bolden has been in the Ministry for over 30 years. Before he became a servant of GOD, he worked as a Break Layer; a profession that he retired from. Prior to that he served his country for 7 years in the United States Air-force.

Dr. Bolden's parents raised him and his three brothers and three sisters in the church serving GOD. He graduated from J.S. Clark High School in 1968 and received a Doctors Degree from Sacramento Theological Seminary Bible College in California in 2012.

On May 12, 2012; Dr. Elbert Bolden was ordain in the office of Apostleship within the Body of Christ through the International World Link Of Churches & Miniseries Incorporated. Prelate Chief Apostle Dr. Lloyd Benson Sr. from Baton Rouge, Louisiana officiated.

GOD lead him to start Liberty Christian Center as the building foundation to his years of ministry. When asked the question, "How many members you have?" Apostle Dr. Elbert Bolden replied, "I don't have members. I make workers in the vein yard, servants of the Kingdom of GOD. We are Disciples of Christ Jesus the Anointed one of GOD. It's all about building a foundation on GOD."

In the beginning
GOD created the
Heaven and the Earth.
Genesis 1:1

75 Messages
Daily Thoughts Of Life

Reverend Doctor Ogden L. King II

(1)
Message:

Much Prayers Much Power, Little Prayer Little Power,
NO Prayer NO Power. There's Power in Prayers.
To: My Awesome Friend in Christ Jesus and your Lovely
Family.

May the blessings of The Lord richly be
with you in Jesus Name Amen!

***** The Words Today *****

Jesus always went to His Father in Prayers
before He took on anything!
To show us How to be Victorious!
The Church Prayed for Peter while he was
in prison and the Angels led him OUT.

Acts 12:5
Peter therefore was kept in prison;
"But" Prayers was made without
ceasing of the church unto GOD for him.
(And he was released)

READ: Acts 12:1 thru 11
Acts 16:25 thru 28

All about POWER in PRAYERS!!!

Trust GOD! I Love You and GOD Love You More!!!

(2)
Message:

HE has risen and paid our sinful debt in full.
Arise and be free!

To: My Awesome Friend in Jesus and your bless Family.
May this Day be Special to You in Jesus Name Amen!

***** The Words Today *****

All I can tell You is He's Risen 2000 plus years ago and
seated at the right hand of The Father for You and I.
So go tell someone.

Matthew 28:6-7
He is not here; for He is risen as He said.
Come, see the place where the Lord lay.
And go quickly, and tell His disciples that
He is risen from the dead,
Rejoice for He has risen.

Love You and GOD Love You More.

(3)
Message:

Jesus Saves!

To: My Bless Friend in the Lord and your Great Family.
May GOD give You the power of Managing
your blessings in Jesus Name Amen!

***** The Words Today *****

Jesus said we can do these works,
"which HE did and Greater! By Faith!!!

John 14:12
Verily, Verily, I say unto you, he that believeth on ME,
the works that I do shall he do also; and Greater works
than these shall he do; because I go unto My Father.

READ: John 14:12 thru 18

GOD left us a Comforter, that
he may abide with us for ever.

Love You and GOD Love You More!!!

(4)
Message:

Why not give yourself to GOD as
He has given His Son for You?

To: My Caring Friend in Christ Jesus and your Anointed
Family. May GOD give You Wisdom Knowledge and
Understanding to worship Him in Spirit and Truth.
Because blessings will Follow.
(First Fruit Time)

***** The Words Today *****

This is the Season that we celebrate when GOD
gave us the ultimate gift, His Son to pay off
sins for us and freedom from the devil.

John 3:16
For GOD so Loved the world that He gave
His only begotten Son, that whosoever believeth
in Him should not Parish, But have everlasting life.

Love You and GOD Love You More!

(5)
Message:

If GOD Words tell you that
You can do it, by Faith you can!

To: My Loving Friend in the Ministry
and your awesome Family.
May the blessings of The Lord Shower You
richly forever in Jesus Name Amen!

***** The Words Today *****

If GOD said that we are conquerors,
It's DONE through Him that Love us!!!

Romans 8:37
Nay, in all these things we are more
than conquerors through Him that Loved us.

READ: Joshua 1:7-8

I can do ALL things through Christ
which Strengthened ME.

Love You and GOD Love You More!!!

(6)
Message:

When we ask GOD for something and
be obedient to HIS words we will
receive from HIM what we ask!

To: My Wonderful Friend in the Body of Christ and
your Beautiful Family. May GOD gives you Wisdom
Knowledge and Understanding to follow
His instructions in Jesus Name Amen!

***** The Words Today *****

In order to receive blessings from GOD
we have to be pleasing to GOD
though His Words by Faith.

1 John 3:22
And whatsoever we ask, we receive of him,
because we keep His commandments,
and do those things that are pleasing in His sight.

READ: 1 John 3:20 thru 24

He said it and can't reversed it.

Love You and GOD Love You More!

(7)
Message:

Remember that GOD will forever be with You!!!
By Faith!

To: My Gracious Friend in the Lord and your Sweet Family.
May GOD opens up your warehouse in
Heaven for You in Jesus Name Amen.

***** The Words Today *****

Keep in mind that GOD is the only one
that will never leave you!!! So let your
conversation be about Him.

Hebrews 13:5
Let your conversation be without covetousness;
and be content with such things as ye have;
for He hath said, I will NEVER leave thee,
nor forsake thee. GOD is everywhere.

READ: Psalms 139:8

Love You and GOD Love You More!

(8)
Message:

If You taste GOD through Faith
You'll see that He's GOOD!

To: My Awesome Friend in the Lord and your Lovely Family.
May GOD make You Healthy Wealthy
and Wise in this Season in Jesus Name Amen!

***** The Words Today *****

You can taste the Lord goodness by trusting in Him by Faith!

Psalm 34:8
O taste and see that the Lord is good.
Blessed is the man that trusteth in Him.

READ: Psalm 34:8 & 9

There is NO WANT to him that fear Him.

IN THE BEGINNING GOD.
He is GOOD all the time!!!

Love You and GOD Love You More!

(9)
Message:

When You follow instructions, that means
the Words of GOD and receive Him
plus believe in His name
You become a child of GOD.

To: My Loving Friend in Christ Jesus
and your Precious Family. May GOD
give You Wisdom Knowledge on how to
be blessed richly forever in Jesus Name. Amen!

***** The Words Today *****

GOD is waiting on us to follow
His Words to become His Children!

John 1:12
But as many as received Him, to them
gave he power to become the sons of GOD,
even to them believe on His name;

READ: John 1:1 thru 14

The Power of GOD is the Holy Spirit.

Love You and GOD Love You More!

❖❖❖❖❖❖❖❖❖❖❖❖❖❖❖❖❖❖❖

(10)
Message:

GOD truly Love us so much to were
He gave His only son for a price to save us!

To: My awesome Friend in the Ministry and
your Anointed Family. May the Mighty
Hands of GOD be on You
richly forever in Jesus Name Amen!!!

***** The Words Today *****

GOD Showed us His Love
by not sparing His Son for us!!!

John 3:16
For GOD so loved the world, that
He gave His only begotten Son,
that whosoever believeth in Him
should not perish, But have everlasting life.

Why not give your life to Him?

Love You and GOD Love You More!

(11)
Message:

Never give up on GOD! Why?
Because He's the only one that
can FIX and SOLVE Anything!!!

To: My Loving Friend in The Word of GOD
and your bless Family. May the Words of
GOD be written on the table of
your Heart in Jesus Name Amen!

***** The Words Today *****

GOD solve Job, Daniel, 3 Hebrew Boys,
Joseph and may others Problems.
He can FIX yours!!! Just follow instructions!
(GOD Words) GOD has Not Changed!!!

Malachi 3:6
For I am the Lord, I change not;
therefore ye sons of Jacob are not consumed.

Trust GOD and You will be Blessed!

Love You and GOD Love You More!

(12)
Message:

GOD will Never Leave You.

To my righteous Friend in the Ministry and
your Great Family. May GOD
guide you to your blessings.

***** The Words Today *****

When You going through trials and
tribulations in Life, GOD will bring
you through it, IF You Trust in His Words!!!

Isaiah 43:2
When thou passest through the waters,
I will be with thee; and through the rivers,
they shall not overflow thee; when thou
walkest through the fire, thou shalt
not be burned; neither shall
the flame kindle upon thee.

No weapon that is formed
against thee shall prosper.
(Isaiah 54:17)

Love You and GOD Love You More.

(13)
Message:

If You woken up this morning
Thank GOD!!!

To: My awesome Friend in the body of Christ
and your Lovely Family. May GOD opens
up the Windows of Heaven and pour you
out blessings You don't have room enough to receive!

***** The Words Today *****

GOD can do MORE than WE can
imagine when we believe in Him!!!

Ephesians 3:20
Now unto Him that is able to do exceeding
abundantly above all that we ask or
think, according to the power that worketh in us.

GOD is not short in anything!!!

Love you and GOD Love You More!!!

(14)
Message:

Come for all GOD Promises or YEA and Amen.
II Corinthians 1:20

To: My Wonderful Friend in the Lord
and your Anointed Family. You're blessed
if You stand on the Words of GOD!
(Instructions)

***** The Words Today *****

If You follow the Words of GOD You shall
Prosper whither-soever thou go-est!
If He did it before He'll do it again for us.

Joshua 1:7
Only be thou strong and very courageous,
that thou mayest observe to do
according to all the law, which Moses
my servant commanded thee; turn not from
it to the right hand or to the left, that
thou may est Prosper whither-soever thou go-est.

All this done by Faith!!!

Love You and GOD Love You More!!!

(15)
Message:

Come and see what GOD has for You.

To: My Precious Friend in the Ministry
and your Awesome Family. May
GOD forever BLESS You richly
this Season in Jesus Name. Amen!!!

***** The Words Today *****

Why not Serve GOD that can
do ALL things except lie!!!

Numbers 23:19
GOD is not a man that He should lie.

Genesis 1:1
IN the beginning GOD created the heaven and the earth.

GOD can FIX ALL our Problems by Faith!
That's a Fact!

Love You and GOD Love You More!

(16)
Message:

This is the Season to help the weak in need!!!

To: My Anointed Friend in the Ministry
and your bless Family. May this Season
be the best you ever had in Jesus Name Amen!

***** The Words Today *****

It is better to give than to receive.

ACTS 20:35
I have shewed you all things; how that so
labouring ye ought to support the weak,
and to remember the Words of the
Lord Jesus, how He said, It is more
blessed to give than to receive.

Father GOD gave His Son for us!

Love You and GOD Love You More.

(17)
Message:

We celebrate this Season of the most
important gift that was given by the Father for us,
HIS Son!

To: My blessed Friend in The Lord and
your Lovely Family. When Praises goes up
blessings comes down! Receive your gifts NOW!!!

***** The Words Today *****

For GOD so loved the world, that He gave
His only begotten Son, that whosoever believeth
in Him should not perish, but have everlasting life.
John 3:16!

Isaiah 9:6
For unto us a child is born, unto us a son is given
and the government shall be upon his shoulder;
and his name shall be called Wonderful,
Counselor, The mighty GOD,
The everlasting Father, The Prince of Peace.

The most Awesome gift of all times Love of GOD.

Love You and GOD Loves You More!
GOD has given us Heavens Best, His Son.

(18)
Message:

Put on the hold armor of GOD
and stand on the Word!

To: My Special Friend in Christ Jesus
and your Anointed Friend. May GOD
meets all your every need this Season
in Jesus Name Amen!

***** The Words Today *****

When You have done all You can just
follow instructions of the Words of GOD
and He shall direct your paths against the devil.

Ephesians 6:11
Put on the whole Armour of GOD,
that ye may be able to stand against
the wiles of the devil.

READ: Ephesians 6:13 thru 18
James 4:7 Joshua 1:1 thru 8

Love You and GOD Love You More!

(19)
Message:

Love one another like Christ first Love us.
Don't let know devil make you hate
your Family in Christ Jesus because he will try.

To my Precious Friend in The Body of Christ and your Lovely
Family. May the Lord bless You richly forever that You never
want are like for nothing ever again in Jesus Name Amen!

***** The Words Today *****
Remember we are never fighting against flesh and blood,
"BUT" against evilness which is from the devil.

Ephesians 6:12
For we wrestle not against flesh and blood,
But against principalities, against power,
against the rulers of the darkness
of this world, against spiritual
wickedness in high places.

READ: Ephesians: 6:12 thru 18 and Matthew: 4:4

Beat the devil with the Words of GOD
GOD is Love!

Love You and GOD Love You More!

(20)
Message:

Trouble don't last always, when You have Jesus!

To: My Joyful Friend in Christ Jesus
and your Anointed Family. May The Lord
make your crooked roads straight
and your ruff roads smooth in Jesus Name.
Amen!

***** The Words Today *****

For His anger endureth "But" a moment;
in His favour is life: weeping may
endure for a night, "But" joy cometh
in the morning. Psalms 30:5

Psalms 34:19
Many are the afflictions of the righteous,
"But" the LORD delivers him out of them all.

No matter what your situation is
keep your Faith in GOD!!!

Love You and GOD Love You More!!!

(21)
Message:

Sometime in Life we think we know more than
the Creator "But" we don't. Be open to be doers
of the Words by Faith.

To: My awesome Friend in The Lord
and your Lovely Family. May the
Heavens opened up and give You
Wisdom in Jesus Name Amen!

***** The Words Today *****
We must open up our Hearts to know
that GOD is the Creator and He knows All.
So follow His Words.

Isaiah 55:8
For my thoughts are not your thoughts,
neither are your ways, saith the Lord.

READ: Isaiah 55:8-9
James 1:22 thru 25

Remember GOD want us to be Blessed.

Love You and GOD Love You More.

(22)
Message:

WITH GOD, You can do ALL THINGS,
through Faith!!! Believe and trust Him.

To: My BLESS Friend in The Lord
and your Wonderful Family. May GOD Shower
You with FAVOR and Blessings. I Speak it in
your life in Jesus Christ Holy Name Amen.

***** The Words Today *****

If GOD Be for You who can be against You!!!
(Romans 8:31)

Luke 1:37
For With GOD nothing shall be impossible.

READ: Jeremiah 32:27

The wonderful thing is He'll never
leave you nor forsake you.

Love You and GOD Love You More!!!

(23)
Message:

If You take care of GOD business,
He'll take care of yours.

To: My unique Friend in The Ministry
and your Anointed Family. May GOD bless You
richly forever in Jesus Name Amen!

***** The Words Today *****

GOD want to bless You and
make You rich and happy!

Proverbs 10:22
The blessing of The Lord, it maketh rich,
and He addeth no sorrow with it.

READ: Deuteronomy 28:2

Blessings will come if You hearken to His voice.

Follow GOD instructions and you will be Blessed.

Love You and GOD Love You More.

(24)
Message:

Call on the name of the
Lord for His Mercy and Grace
to direct your Soul to GLORY.

To: My Awesome Friend in The Ministry
and your Anointed Family. May the light of
GOD continue to shine on You in Jesus Name Amen.

***** The Words Today *****

GOD Words are True and Just.
So why not call on Him to save you.

Romans 10:13
For whosoever shall call upon the
name of the Lord shall be saved.

READ: Joel 2:32
Why wait? Do these things by Faith.

Love You and GOD Love You More.

(25)
Message:

He that keepeth his mouth keepeth his life
(But) he that openeth wide his lips
shall have destruction.
(Proverbs 13:3)

To: My bless Friend in The Lord and your Wonderful Family.
May the Holy Spirit direct your paths in Jesus Name Amen!

***** The Words Today *****
Proverbs 18:21
Death and life (are) in the power of the tongue and they that
Love it shall eat the fruit thereof. (Watch Negative talk)

Matthew 12:36
But I say unto you, That every idle word that man shall
speak, they shall give account thereof in the day of judgment.

READ: 1 Peter 3:10, Proverbs: 15:1, James 3:8
(For people like me)
James 1:26

Pray for me and I'll Pray for You.

Love You and GOD Love You More.

(26)
Message:

GOD holds our Destiny in His Hands,
so why not serve Him?

To: My Loving Friend in the Ministry and
your Anointed Family. May GOD order
your foot steps in Jesus Name Amen!

***** The Words Today *****

If GOD knows all things,
why not trust Him.
If GOD be for you
who can be against you?

1 John 3:20
For if our heart condemn us, GOD
is greater than our heart and knoweth all things.

READ: Psalm 139:1-4, Matthew 10:30, Psalm 147:4

Remember Trust GOD.

Love You and GOD Love You More!!!

(27)
Message:

Come together with Faith in Agreement
and watch GOD moves in your Life!

To: My Precious Friend in Christ Jesus
and your Lovely Family. May the kingdom
of GOD shower You with FAVOR
this Season in Jesus Name!!!

***** The Words Today *****
There's Power in Agreement when we unify our self
with Faith in the walk with GOD by two (2).

Matthew 18:19
Again I say unto you, That if two of You
shall agree on earth as touching any thing
that they shall ask, it shall be done
for them of my Father which is in heaven.

(READ verse 20 also)

Remember this is the Words of GOD
and His Words are TRUE!

Love You and GOD Love You more

(28)
Message:

If GOD says You are blessed He can't reverse it.

To: My Caring Friend in the Ministry
and your Beautiful Family. May the Lord
Shower You with all your desires in Jesus Name Amen.

***** The Words Today *****

Speak Blessings in your life because
GOD has already prepared it for You!

Numbers 23:20
Behold, I have received commandment
to bless; and He hath blessed; and I cannot reverse it.

Genesis 1:28
And GOD blessed them,

(READ 1:26,27 & 28).

Remember this GOD can't lie!

Love You and GOD Love You more!

(29)
Message:

Bring GOD with You where ever
you go and you will overcome.

To: My Beautiful Friend in Christ Jesus
and your Sweet Family. May
GOD forever give You Strength and
Favor in your walk with GOD.

***** The Words Today *****

Nothing is to hard for GOD that
gave His Son for us! That's Love!

Roman 8:31, 32
What shall we then say to these things?
If GOD be for us, who can be against us?
He that spared not His own Son, But delivered
Him up for us all, how shall He not with
Him also freely give us all things?

Living for GOD is a life style.

Love You and GOD Love You more

(30)
Message:

If You need it GOD got it.
Just put Him first in your Life!

To: My joyful Friend in Christ Jesus and your Beautiful
Family. May the blessings of the Lord forever be with
You richly in Jesus Name Amen.

***** The Words Today *****

Remember it's GOD that gives Power
to get Wealth to establish His covenant.

Deuteronomy 8:18
But thou shalt remember the Lord thy
GOD for it is He that giveth thee Power
to get Wealth, that He may establish
His covenant which He sware unto thy
father, as it is this Day.

Delight yourself also in the Lord and
He will give You the desires of your heart.

Love You and GOD Love You more!

(31)
Message:

Keep your Heart and Mind
on Jesus The Christ.

To: My Loving Friend in The Word
of GOD and your Awesome Family.
May Father GOD forever BLESS
You in Jesus Name Amen!

***** The Words Today *****

Our Purpose is to go out and preach
the Gospel through out the World!
Remember GOD got You!

Mark 16:15
And He said unto them, Go ye into
ALL the World and Preach the
Gospel to every creature.

Follow GOD instructions and
You shall truly be Blessed!

Love You and GOD Love You more!!!

(32)
Message:

GOD is not a man that He should lie.

To: My Wonderful Friend in the Ministry
and your Beautiful Family May the
Mighty Hands of GOD be upon
You richly forever in Jesus Name Amen!
(FAVOR)

***** The Words Today *****
GOD Words will not go out and
come back void. It will do exactly
what it say it's going to do.

Isaiah 55:11
So shall my word be that goeth forth
out of my mouth; it shall not return
unto me void, But it shall Accomplish
that which I Please, and it shall Prosper
in the things where to I sent it.

Remember trust in GOD.

Love You and GOD Love You more.

(33)
Message:

Keep Jesus near to your Heart.

To: My Anointed Friend or Wife
in the Lord and your Lovely Family.
May the blessings of the Lord be upon
You forever in Jesus Name Amen!

***** The Words Today *****

Once You except Jesus, the greater
one dwell in You and that gives
You power over the devil.

1 John 4:4
Ye are of GOD, little children and
have overcome them: because greater
is he that is in You, then he that
is in the world.

Remember that You have the power to speak
blessings in your life NOW by Faith.

Love You and GOD Love You more.

(34)
Message:

Keep your hands in the Master Hands
which is Jesus and watch
Him Work in your life.

To: My blessed Friend or Wife in
The Ministry and your Sweet
Darling Family. May GOD shower
You richly forever with favor
in Jesus Name Amen.

***** The Words Today *****

No matter what you going through
in Life rather it's good or bad
GOD will never leave you.

Hebrews 13:5
Let your conversation be without
covetousness; and be content with
such things as ye have; for He hath
said (I will never leave thee, nor forsake thee).

READ: Hebrews 13:5 thru 8

Love You and GOD Love You more

(35)
Message:

Beat the devil with the Words of GOD!

To: My Anointed Friend in the Lord
and your Lovely Family. May GOD
give you favor above measures
in Jesus Name Amen!!!

***** The Words Today *****

Jesus showed us how to defeat the devil
and that's with the Words of GOD.

Matthew 4:4
But He answered and said, It is written,
Man shall not live by bread alone "but"
by every word that proceedeth
out of the mouth of GOD.

READ: Joshua ch 1: 7-8

Do what Jesus tell You to do and
you shall be Blessed abundantly!

I Love You & GOD Love You more.

(36)
Message:

Put GOD first in your life!

To: My Wonderful Friend in the
Ministry and your Beautiful Family.
May GOD Shine His Loving lights on
You forever in Jesus Name Amen!!!
Thanks for allowing me to be
apart of the Family.

***** The Words Today *****

GOD will give you the desires of your
heart if you follow His Instructions!!!

Psalm 37:4
Delight thyself also in the Lord
and He shall give thee the
desires of thine heart.

READ: Psalms 37:4-5.

Love You and GOD Love You more!

(37)
Message:

Stand on the Words of GOD
and you shall see blessings.

To: My bless Friends in The Ministry and your Lovely
Family. May the blessings of the Lord Shower
You richly in Jesus Name Amen.

***** The Words Today *****
GOD Words is true and just,
so you can stand on it
until all is fulfilled.

Matthew 5:18
For verily I say unto you,
till heaven and Earth pass,
one jot or one tittle shall in
no wise pass from the law,
till all be fulfilled.

READ: Matthew 5:17-18
Malachi 3:6
Hebrews 13:8

Love You and GOD Love You more!

(38)
Message:

Thou shalt have no other
GODs before Him
(Exodus 20:3-5)

To: My Loving Friend in The Lord
and your Lovely Family. May the
blessings of the Lord Shower
You richly in Jesus Name Amen.

***** The Words Today *****

Always Trust in GOD not your
ways and He shall direct thy paths.

Proverbs 3:5
Trust in the Lord with all thine
heart and lean not unto thine
own understanding.

READ: Proverbs 3:5 thru 10

Much Love to You and yours

Remember, GOD Love You more!

(39)
Message:

GOD is a re-warder to
those that diligently seek Him.
Hebrews 11:6

To: My outstanding Friend in the Ministry and your
wonderful Family. May GOD shower You with Wisdom
Knowledge and Understanding in Jesus Name Amen!!!

***** The Words Today *****
If You seek GOD you shall find Him.
Follow instructions with Faith
and ask you shall be given.

Matthew 7:7
Ask and it shall be given you;
seek and ye shall find; knock,
and it shall be opened unto you.

READ: Hebrews 11:6

Continue to seek GOD

Love You and GOD Love You more.

(40)
Message:

Thou shalt have no other GODs before me.
(Exodus 20:3)

To: My Anointed Friend in the Gospel and your Lovely Family.
May the Holy Spirit guide your way in Jesus Name!

***** The Words Today *****
Jesus said none good but GOD him self. So why
Judge People. That's Jesus Job so pick up your
cross and follow Jesus He will show us
Great and Mighty Things!!!

Mark 10:18 (Read Mark 10:17-25)
And Jesus said unto him why callest thou me good?
There is none good but one, that is GOD.

Luke 6:37
Judge not, and ye shall not be judge; condemn not, and
ye shall not be condemned; forgive, and ye shall be forgiven:
Read Numbers 23:19

GOD is not a man that He should lie.

It's GOD words!
Love You and GOD Love You more!!!

(41)
Message:

You not waiting for GOD,
GOD is waiting for You!

To: My Loving Friend in the Ministry and
your beautiful Family. May the blessings
of the Lord Shower You this Season!!!

***** The Words Today *****
If Jesus tell You to do something,
just do it. There is a reward coming.

Matthew 5: 44
But I say unto you, Love your enemies,
bless them that curse you, do good to
them that hate you, and pray for them
which despitefully use you, and persecute you;
That ye may be the children of
your Father which is in heaven;

READ Matthew 5:44 thru 48

Love You and Bless GOD forever!

(42)
Message:

Make GOD First in your life.

To: My Anointed Wife in the Spirit
and our precious Family. I speak
blessings in your life in Jesus
Christ Holy Name Amen!!!

***** The Words Today *****
When You trust GOD He shall protect
You from all evil things through Faith!!!

Romans 8:31-32
What shall we then say to these things?
If GOD be for us, who can be against us?

Isaiah 54:17
No weapon that is formed
against thee shall prosper;

Love You with Action.

May the Power of the Holy Spirit be upon
You forever in Jesus Name Amen!

Message:

Let Jesus be your guide in
Life and you shall be Blessed!!!

To: My Marvelous Friend in The Lord
and our Wonderful Family. May GOD
bless You richly in every areas of your
life in Jesus Christ Holy Name Amen.

***** The Words Today *****

Trouble don't last always when
Joy is knocking at your Door
through Christ Jesus!

Psalms 30:5
For His anger endureth but a moment;
in His favour is life: weeping may endure
for a night, but joy cometh in the morning.

Love You with the Love of GOD
with Action in Jesus Name Amen!!!

(44)
Message:

Pentecost today! Put GOD First in
your life and watch the blessings Flow.

To: My Loving Wife in Christ Jesus and
our Lovely Family. May GOD opens
up the Windows of Favor on your life
in Jesus Christ Holy Name Amen. (By Faith)

***** The Words Today *****

Don't worry if you are going through
the storms of life if you have Jesus,
Because the Lord will bring you out of it all.

Psalm 34:19
Many are the afflictions of the righteous
"But" the Lord delivereth him out of them all.

READ: Psalm 34:20 thru 22

Love You with action
the way Jesus first Love us.

(45)
Message:

GOD Goes First!!!
To: My Wonderful Friends in Christ Jesus even though
you gave up on us and Sweet Darling Family.
May GOD forever watch over You in Jesus Name Amen!

***** The Words Today *****
When Jesus returns will he
find Faith and Love on the Earth?

Luke 18:8
I tell you that he will avenge them speedly.
Nevertheless; when the son of man cometh,
shall he find Faith on the earth?

READ John 13:34/ 1John 4:20-21/ Matthew 5:44
Genesis 18:16-32/ Proverbs 10:12/ Matthew 24:12.

So don't say you Love someone and don't show Action.

Love You with the Love of GOD and
may HE give you Mercy, Grace and
Favor forever more in Jesus name.

(46)
Message:

I Repeat, Put GOD First Amen!!!

To: My Adorable Friends in Christ Jesus and our
Beautiful Family. May the blessings of the Lord res
upon You richly forever in Jesus Christ Holy Name Amen.

***** The Words Today *****

My Strength is made perfect
in weakness through GOD Grace!!!

II Corinthians 12:9
And He said unto me, My Grace is
sufficient for thee; for my strength is
made perfect in weakness. Most
gladly therefore will I rather glory
in my infirmities that the
Power of Christ may rest upon me.

May GOD give Grace & Favor unto You.

Love You and GOD Love You
more in Jesus Name Amen.

(47)
Message:

Mighty Woman of GOD you will be Blessed!!!

To: My Anointed Friends in the Gospel
and our Precious Family. May
GOD continue to bless You richly.

***** The Words Today *****

Obey your Mother & your Father
and your life May be long on the Earth!

Ephesians 6:1thru 3
Children obey your parents in
the Lord for this is right.

Honour thy father and mother, which
is the commandment with promises.
That it may be well with thee, and
thou mayest live long on the Earth.

Love You all and GOD Love You more!!!

Bring a Friend today.

(48)
Message:

MEMO!!!
Be Obedient and put GOD First in your life!
May Blessings be upon you richly.

To: My Anointed Friend that GOD gave me and your
Lovely Family. May GOD hands stay upon You
in Jesus Christ Holy Name Amen.

***** The Words Today *****

If you want Reward on Earth
have Faith, Believing and Diligently seek GOD.

Hebrews 11:6
But without Faith it is impossible to please Him; for
He that cometh to GOD must believe that He is,
and that He is a rewarder of them that diligently seek Him.

Read: Isaiah 55:6

Love You and May the blessings
of the Lord continue being with You.
Remember keep speaking Positive.

(49)
Message:

Remember, Let's put GOD First
in our life and He shall bless You.

To: My Loving Sister in the Gospel and your Precious
Family. May GOD blessings be with You!

***** The Words Today *****
Be careful on what you say out of your mouth!!!

Proverbs 6:2
Thou art snared with the words
of thy mouth, thou art taken
with the words of thy mouth.

Read: Proverbs 18:21/Genesis 1:26

Remember family of Christ Jesus we are
made in GOD image and His likeness.
So be careful on what comes out of the mouth,
Positive or Negative words.

GOD Love You and I Love You too.

(50)
Message:

You want to be obedient TO GOD?
Make it to the House of Prayers.
Put GOD First in your life and
watch your blessings OVER FLOW!!!

To: My precious Child in the Lord and our Loving
Family. Keep trusting GOD and His Words and
You shall be Blessed!!!

***** The Words Today *****
Who you going to trust
The Lord or man.

Psalms 118:8
It is better to trust in the Lord than
to put confidence in man.

READ: Numbers 24:19/ Malachi 3:6
Matthew 5:18/ Hebrews 13:8

Remember to speak positive and
put GOD First and watch Him
OVER FLOW you with blessings.

(51)
Message:

Let's celebrate the rising of
Christ Jesus The Son of GOD.

To: My Wonderful Friends and years Friendship
in Christ Jesus and our Outstanding Families!!!

***** The Words Today *****
This is the Day we celebrate the Rising
of our Savior Jesus who over came the World.

Luke 24:46
And said unto them, Thus it is written,
and thus it behoved Christ to suffer,
and to rise from the dead the third DAY;

Remember body of Christ, because what Jesus did for
us we can NOW have the desire of Our Heart and eternal
life. So tell Jesus what you need and want.

GOD Love You and I Love You too.

In the Name of The Father The Son
and The Holy Spirit Amen.

(52)
Message:

It works! Obedient is better than Sacrifice.
Let's do it again and be Blessed!!

To: Our Beautiful Family. Continue to hold
onto GOD unchanging Hands. Remember
to always Speak Positive in your life!

***** The Words Today *****

You are free so Love and serve one
another like Jesus did in the Spirit.

Galatians 5:13
For, brethren, ye have been called unto liberty;
only use liberty for an occasion to the flesh,
but by Love serve one another.

READ: Galatians 5:13 thru 26

Remember GOD is Love so Love one
another as He first Love You.

Love you and Be Blessed.

(53)
Message:

Remember Faith come by hearing.
BE at Church for your blessing!

To: My Wonderful Family. May
GOD continue to shines His Loving Light
on you in Jesus Christ Holy Name Amen!!!

***** The Words Today *****

If Jesus says Do it, then Do it and don't Doubt!

Mark 11:22
And Jesus answering saith unto them,
Have Faith in GOD.

READ: Mark 11:22 thru 26

Love You and
May the blessings
of GOD Be upon
You forever!

(54)
Message:

May the Loving Hands of GOD be upon you to bring you
Protection and Favor forever in Our Lord and
Savior Jesus Christ Holy Name Amen!!!

To: Our Blessed Family in the Ministry.

***** The Words Today *****
When nothing else will Stand for us,
GOD words will Stand True forever.

Isaiah 40:8
The grass witherth, the flowers fadeth
"But" the word of our GOD shall stand for ever.

Proverbs 3:5
Trust in the Lord with all thine Heart,
and lean not unto thine own understanding.

READ: Proverbs 3:5 thru 10

It's never too late with GOD!!!

Love You with the Love of GOD.
May the precious Blood and the
Power of the Holy Spirit be with You always.

(55)
Message:

May GOD open up your Heart to receive Wisdom and
Favor. I ask The Father in Jesus Christ Holy Name Amen!

To: My Wonderful Family in the Gospel.

***** The Words Today *****
The Bible says
Malachi 3:6 For I am the Lord I change not;

Hebrews 13:8 Jesus Christ the same yesterday,
and today, and for ever.

Number 23:20 Behold, I have received commanded to bless,
and He hath blessed; and I cannot Reverse it.
(So follow Instructions and watch GOD move by Faith)

Matthew 7:7
Ask, and it shall be given you; seek, and
ye shall find; knock, and it shall be open unto you.

Have Faith in GOD because its nothing to hard for
GOD because He can meet all your every need.

GOD Loves you and I Love You too.

(56)
Message:

May the Power of The Holy Spirit be upon you as
you follow Instructions in Jesus Christ Holy Name
Amen! Miss You already, still not to late
if you let GOD have His way.

To:Our Lovely Family.

***** The Words Today *****
Faith Multiplies Your Blessings!
Jesus take a little and your Faith makes it alot.

Matthew 14:19
And He commanded the multitude to sit
down on the grass, and took the five loaves,
and the two fishes, and looking up to heaven,
He blessed, and brake, and gave the loaves to
His disciples, and the disciples to the multitude.
(He Fed them all)

Read: Matthew 14:13 thru 21
Matthew 18:19, Hebrews 11:6
(Faith Pleases GOD)

Love You and keep the Faith

(57)
Message:

I Pray the blessings of GOD Be upon you
and your Family richly forever. I ask this
in Jesus Christ Holy Name Amen!

To: Your Lovely Family.

***** The Words Today *****
Remember! Because you're not of this world,
it Treats you Bad sometimes. Don't fear,
the world know Jesus not. That's because
we are children of GOD by His Love
thru our Faith, and His Grace.

1 John 3:1
BEHOLD, what manner of Love the Father hath bestowed
upon us, that we should be called the sons of GOD;
therefore the world knoweth us
not, because it know Him not.

READ 1 John 3:1 & 2

GOD Love You and I Love You too. I'm in Agreement
with you as it Reads in Matthew 18:19 and GOD
words don't lie.

Keep The Faith!!!

(58)
Message:

May the blessings of GOD and Favour
over Flow you from Heaven. I ask
The Father this in Jesus Christ Holy Name Amen!

GOD is showing us signs and wonders.
We are truly blessed. Keep the Faith My Love

To: My Anointed Friends in the Lord,
and Their Wonderful Families.

***** The Words Today *****
GOD is Faithful to His Promises

Hebrews 10:23
Let us hold fast the Profession of
our Faith without wavering;
(for He is Faithful that Promised:)

Read: Numbers 23:19 /// Matthews 11:28 thru 30

(All of this by Faith!!!)
Remember GOD words are true and just, so what ever
your needs are," make sure you put Him first
and He shall meet all your needs.

GLORY to GOD Love You and BE BLESSED!!!

(59)
Message:

May the Power of GOD be on you
all with Favour in Jesus Christ
Holy Name Amen. Don't let Satan
destroy our Hearts What Jesus has fixed Okay!

To: My Wonderful Beautiful Family.

***** The Words Today *****

Christ Jesus is able to do exceeding,
abundantly above all that
we ask or think, By Faith.

Ephesians 3:20
Now unto Him that is able to do
exceeding abundantly above all that
we ask or think, according to the
Power that worketh in us.

Remember GOD can meet all your
every and any needs by Faith.

Love You all and continue to trust GOD.

(60)
Message:

May GOD open up the Windows of Heaven
and pour you out a blessing you don't
have room to receive by Faith. I ask
The Father this in Jesus Christ Holy Name Amen!

To: GOD Faithful servant and our Lovely Family.

***** The Words Today *****
If GOD said it stand on it.
He shall direct thy paths by Faith!

PROVERBS 3:5,6
Trust in the Lord with all thine heart;
and lean not unto thine own understanding.
In all thy ways acknowledge Him,
and He shall direct thy Paths.

READ: Proverbs 3:5 thru 10

Love You and continue to follow GOD
Instructions by Faith and you will
see the movement of GOD!
For GOD be the GLORY!

(61)
Message:

I Pray that GOD anointing be upon you richly forever
in Jesus Christ Holy Name Amen! As I am yours
U R mind! Don't let no one change that.

To Our Bless Family.

***** The Words Today *****
GOD is waiting on You not you waiting on GOD.
He wants to Show You Great and Mighty
Things Don't wait, call onto Him "Now!"

Jeremiah 33:3
Call unto Me, and I will answer thee,
and shew thee Great and Mighty
Things, which thou knowest not.

Love You with the Love of GOD and
continue to be blessed by Faith.

Remember
Psalms 102:13
this season mercy & favour by Faith.

(62)
Message:

May the Lord over Flow you with
Wisdom and Favour by Faith!!!

I'm in agreement with you in
Jesus Christ Holy Name Amen!!!

To: GOD Faithful servant and our Lovely Family.

***** The Words Today *****
Troubles don't last always in
Christ Jesus by Faith.

Psalms 30:5
For His anger endureth
"But" a moment; in His Favour is life:
Weeping may endure for a night
"But" joy cometh in the morning.

In GOD Favour is life!

GOD Love You and we Love You too.

Continue to let Jesus bless you by Faith.

(63)
Message:

Lets try one more time so
Jesus can work again in Our life.

To: Our Beautiful Family. May the blessings of
The Lord be upon you richly and
forever in Jesus Christ Holy Name Amen!!!

***** The Words Today *****
Jesus showed us how to defeat the devil while He was
here on earth With The Words of GOD!!!

Matthew 4:4
But He answered and said, It is written,
Man shall not live by bread alone, "But" by every
word that proceedeth out of the mouth of GOD.

(Read) Matthew 3:15,16
Matthew 4:1 thru 11

Family in Christ remember Psalms 102:13. Zion
meaning Church get ready in this season for
mercy and Favour is come meaning Now.

Only if you have Faith, because Faith pleases GOD.
Love You and be blessed!!!

(64)
Message:

May GOD shower you abundantly with
Mercy and Favor forever more I ask
The Father this in Jesus Christ Holy Name Amen!!!

To: My Wonderful Parter,
"if" you still Love me and our Beautiful Family.

***** The Words Today *****
Because what Jesus did for us on the Cross, "Now" we
can do all things By Faith, Though Christ Jesus!!!
(Your Faith Have Made You Hold)!!! Amen.

Philippians 4:13
I can do all things through Christ which strengthens me.

Proverbs 8:10,11
Receive my Instructions, and not Silver; and Knowledge
rather than choice Gold. For Wisdom is better than Rubies:

Remember Family in Christ Jesus Instructions,
Knowledge and Wisdom is valuable through Faith.

Love You and May GOD continue to bless you
richly in Jesus Christ Holy Name Amen!!!

(65)
Message:

I speak Wisdom and Blessings upon you all
this Season and forever more in The Name
of The Father The Son and The Holy Spirit Amen.

I Think GOD for allowing us to touch and agree as a Family.
There is Power! GLORY TO GOD!!!

To: my Beautiful Sweet Wife
and our Lovely Sweet Family

***** The Words Today *****
No matter what troubles you go through GOD Will bring
you out of it and have mercy and give you favor!!!

Psalms 34:19
Many are the afflictions of the righteous,
"But the Lord delivers him out of them all.

Read
Psalms 34:13 thru 19 Psalms 102:13

Remember stand on those words by Faith.
Love you and may the blessing of GOD
continue to be with you forever in
Jesus Christ Holy Name Amen!!!

(66)
Message:

We Pray that you receive the blessings in every areas
of your life in Jesus Christ Holy Name Amen!!!

To: Our beloved Friends and Family
in the Ministry, our Kids and grandkids.
On behalf of Liberty Christian Center
we would like to thank you for allowing us
in your home with the Words of GOD.

***** The Words Today *****
If you ask anything by Faith,
GOD Will give it to you.

Matthew 7:7
Ask, and it shall be given you; seek,
and ye shall find; knock, and
it shall be opened unto you:

Remember 7 is GOD number of completion.
So be in expectation for multitude of blessing.
I want to receive texts of testimony
of the Goodness of GOD.

Love you and be richly blessed in The Name
of The Father The Son and The Holy Spirit Amen.

(67)
Message:

Blessed be to you and your Wonderful family

To: My Friend Woman of GOD

***** The Words Today *****
Psalm 150: 6
Let every thing that hath breath Praise the Lord.
Praise the Lord. Now Praise release Spiritual Authority.
When you Praise GOD he release Power unto you.

Read: Act 16: 25, 26

It tells how Paul and Silas Prayed and Sang
Praises to GOD and He showed up for them.

Remember GOD will do the same for us
when we Praise Him and He'll meet our Needs.

Glory to GOD
May the blessings of GOD be upon you and your family
forever more in the Name of The Father The Son
and The Holy Spirit Amen

Love you all in GOD the Father thru Jesus.

(68)
Message:

May the blessings of GOD shower you all with
Wisdom Knowledge and Understanding
also make you Healthy Wealthy and Wise
in Our Lord and Savior Jesus Christ Holy Name Amen!!!

To: My Friend and Minister of GOD
Words and your Loving Family.

***** The Words Today *****

Philippians 4:13
I can do all things through Christ which strengthen me.

Philippians 4:19
But my GOD shall supply all your needs according
to His riches in Glory by Christ Jesus. Remember
GOD will meet all your needs if you continue
to have faith and believe in His Loving Words.

May the Peace of Christ Jesus be
in your Heart for EVER Amen.

Love you all and be blessed on this day of Worship.

Friend of GOD

(69)
Message:

Remember the Word Favor.

To: The Mighty Man and Woman of GOD,
my Brothers, Sisters and Friends in
Christ Jesus forever more and your family.

***** The Words for Today *****

Glory to GOD

May the blessings of GOD bless you and
your family abundantly in
Jesus Christ Holy Name Amen.

Love to all of you,
my Brothers, Sisters and Friends!!!

(70)
Message:

May the blessings of GOD continue to
be with you forever more. I ask The Father this in
Jesus Christ Holy Name Amen!!!

To: A wonderful Child of GOD and My Anointed Family.

***** The Words Today *****
GOD have much more for you "If" you Love Him!!!

1 Corinthian 2:9
But as it is written, EYES HATH NOT SEEN,
NOR EAR HEARD, NEITHER HAVE
ENTERED INTO THE HEART OF MAN,
THE THINGS WHICH GOD HATH PREPARED
FOR THEM THAT LOVE HIM!!!

John 19:30
It Is Finished! Keep Following GOD Instructions
and He shall meet all of your needs.

Love you my Dear and may GOD give you
Favor in Jesus name Amen, stay blessed.

Thanks for being You!!!
Anointed Woman of GOD

(71)
Message:

We Are Blessed

To: My Anointed beautiful Partner
and our beautiful Family.

May The Father open up the Windows of Heaven
and Shower you this Season above measure.
I ask The Father this in Jesus Christ Holy Name Amen.

***** The Words Today *****

GOD is not a man that He should lie;
If His words say it and you believe
and have Faith it shall come to Pass.

Proverbs 13:22
A good man leave an inheritance to his
children's children; and the Wealth
of the Sinner is laid up for the Just.
This is the Season to Celebrate Our Savior
Jesus The Christ every day and forever more.

Love you and keep Praising Him.

We are Mighty Partners of GOD

(72)
Message:

Season to Rejoice

To: The Family of Christ Jesus
I like to wish all a Merry Christmas
(Christ Day).

***** The Words Today *****
The Savior Came, He Payed our Debt In Full,
And Now We Are Saved By Faith!

*****Glory To GOD*****

Isaiah 9:6
For unto us a child is born, unto us a Son is given:
and the government shall be upon His shoulder
and His name shall be called Wonderful, Counselor,
The Mighty GOD, The everlasting Father,
The Prince of Peace.

Love you and be blessed this Season
and forever more in Jesus Christ Holy Name
Amen.

(73)
Message:

Have a blesseth day to you,
and your family which
GOD Loves and I Love too.

May the blessings of GOD
be upon all of you
forever more starting now in
Jesus Christ Holy Name
Amen!!!

***** The Words for Today *****

GOD Never Break His Word And
He Give Us Dominion And
He Never Change.

Ask and you shell receive the Glory to GOD.

May He bless you abundantly and
your family in all areas of your life
in Jesus Holy Name Amen.

I Love you all from the heart my Friend.

(74)
Message:

To: My Wonderful Friend in the Body of Christ
What a Great morning to you and your Lovely family.

***** The Words for today *****
No matter how hard life might seem
or what trouble you might go through
or when you might feel down and out.
GOD Mercy Endureth forever,
Glory to GOD.

GOD will bring you through what ever
Storms you go through!!!
He is a great and just GOD and He
Love us so much. All we have to do is
Believe and have Faith Amen.

May the Lord bless you abundantly with
Wisdom Knowledge and Understanding.
And may GOD make you Healthy Wealthy
and Wise in Jesus Christ Holy Name Amen.

Much Love my Friend and I thank GOD
for the work that He let you do. Amen!!!

(75)
Message:

Believe

To: All followers of the Gospel

***** The Words for Today *****
Praise ye the Lord and Savior and GOD will take care
of you and all of your needs.

No matter how big or how small the Problem
He can fix it "If you Believe".

Glory to GOD May GOD continue to do a great work
in you and bless you abundantly with
Wisdom Knowledge and Understanding
and heal you from the crown of your head
to the Soul of your feet and bless you
richly in Jesus Christ Holy and
Wonderful Name Amen!!!

Love you and GOD bless you abundantly
Mighty Man of GOD Amen!!!!!

You are my Friend and my Brother!!!!!!!!
Praise GOD

Special Thanks

First: I would like to Thank GOD All Mighty for bringing me through my trials and tribulations. By standing on the words of GOD I have no regrets about the path I went through for my predestine life. GOD's Word will go out and not come back void with blessings.

Second: I would like to thank Mr. and Mrs. Charles Manns for prepping me up for the past 30 plus years for a time like this. It took much "grooming up" to turn some young country boys into the men we are today.

Third: I would like to thank Apostle Dr. Elbert Bolden for believing in me and putting up with me for the past 20 plus years. Remember that GOD has your back, front, side, top, and bottom. We serve an awesome GOD and there is nothing too hard for our GOD.

Fourth: I would like to thank the Bodies of Christ at Liberty Christian Center for allowing me to teach the Gospel for the past 11 years. II Corinthians 5:17 says, "Therefore if any man be in Christ, he is a new creature: old things are passed away; behold all things become new."

Fifth: I would like to thank Evangelist Pearlie Johnson for being a mother and preparing me for my walk with GOD and all my friends and family who respect the calling on my life.

Last, But Not Least: My kids and grand-kids. I Love You All.

COME

Worship With Us

Liberty Christian Center
1229 West Landry Street
Opelousas, LA 70570

Pastor
REVEREND DOCTOR OGDEN L. KING II
ogdenlukeking@gmail.com

Friendship

**REVEREND DOCTOR OGDEN L. KING II
and
APOSTLE DOCTOR ELBERT BOLDEN**

A Friend is something Special, because Jesus calls us His Friend. John 15:13 says "Greater Love hath no man that he lay down his life for his Friends". In the book of John 15:14 Jesus said "Ye are my Friends, if ye do whatsoever I command you". Apostle Dr. Elbert Bolden is my friend. Over 20 years ago he followed the instructions of GOD that prophesied that I would someday have a ministry serving the Lord. Due to the friendship, mentorship, leadership and guidance of Apostle Dr. Elbert Bolden this prophecy has come to pass.

I meet Apostle Dr. Elbert Bolden when I was 15 years old and he was on leave from the United Staes Airforce. He was always a man that would tell it like it is. I knew right away he had the right 4 letters in his last name. "Bold". One thing I learn from him is that the truth hurts. However, if it lines up with the Word of God it will get you through pain and through life. Apostle Dr. Elbert Bolden became my mentor and brought me to except Christ as my Lord and Savior. I now Pastor and Teach the Word of GOD because of My Friend, Apostle Dr. Elbert Bolden.

These are my two Brothers in Christ Jesus that fight against the devil with the power of GOD to direct God people back to Him.

From Left to Right – Rev. Dr. Ogden I. King II, apostle Dr. Elbert Bolden and Minister Refial Papillion.

Rev. Dr. Ogden L. King II giving some inspirational words to a woman of God that Love the Lord faithful to Him.

Sister Ira Jean Milton

Just open up in prayer for a family gathering to deliver some encouraging words in a trouble times like no

From Left to Right – Brother Wilton J. King Jr., Sister Lou-Ann Boutte in Christ Jesus and of course Rev. Dr. Ogden L. Kingg II.

Me and my Brothers getting ready for Spiritual warfare as we get ready to present God's Words. Remember the words of God is more powerful than any weapon!

Hebrews 4:12 – For the word of God is quick and powerful, and sharper than any two – edged sword, piercing even to the diving asunder of soul and spirit, and of the joints and marrow, and is a discerner of the thought and intents of the heart.

From Left to Right – Rev. Dr. Ogden L. King II, apostle Dr. Elbert Bolden and Minister Refial Papillion.

This is The Gospel Group call G.K.G.L. SPIRIT that has been together for 20 plus years bringing forth God's Words in songs and Praises. The G.K.G.L. stands for God's Kingdom God's Love.

Remember it's all about Glorifying God Mighty Name Amen.

From Left to Right - Rev. Dr. Kip K. Guilbeau (Nephew), Rev. Dr. Ogden L. King II, brother Calvin C. Guilbeau (Nephew) and Brother Dale Lavergne (Friend).

Here I am Rev. Dr. Ogden L. King II sitting and thanking God for using me for His Glory. It is an honor to be a Servant of God. God is still in the miracle working business. I was in a wheelchair twice and couldn't do for myself. I had to learn how to walk, talk and use my hands all over again and God Prevail for me by Faith, because Faith Pleases God.

Hebrews 11:6 – but without faith it is impossible to please him: for he that cometh to God must believe that he is, and he is, and that he is rewarder of them that diligently seek him.

In Closing my Brothers and Sisters Believe and keep the Faith. He did it for me, he will do it for you.

God Words can't lie!
Love You And God Love You More!